The Best of The MAILBOX Magazine

Pumpkins

grades PreK–K

Our best pumpkin activities and reproducibles from the 2000–2011 issues of *The Mailbox* and *Teacher's Helper* magazines

- Literacy activities
- Learning centers
- Group-time activities
- Songs
- Math activities
- Arts-and-crafts ideas
- …and more!

Fun and practical skills practice!

Managing Editor: Brenda Fay

Editorial Team: Becky S. Andrews, Diane Badden, Kimberley Bruck, Karen A. Brudnak, Pam Crane, Chris Curry, David Drews, Tazmen Fisher Hansen, Marsha Heim, Lori Z. Henry, Mark Rainey, Greg D. Rieves, Hope Rodgers-Medina, Rebecca Saunders, Donna K. Teal, Sharon M. Tresino, Zane Williard

www.themailbox.com

©2013 The Mailbox® Books
All rights reserved.
ISBN 978-1-61276-371-2

Except as provided for herein, no part of this publication may be reproduced or transmitted in any form or by any means, electronic or mechanical, including photocopying, recording, or storing in any information storage and retrieval system or electronic online bulletin board, without prior written permission from The Education Center, LLC. Permission is given to the original purchaser to reproduce pages for individual classroom use only and not for resale or distribution. Reproduction for an entire school or school system is prohibited. Please direct written inquiries to The Education Center, LLC, PO Box 9753, Greensboro, NC 27429-0753. The Education Center®, *The Mailbox*®, the mailbox/post/grass logo, and The Mailbox Book Company® are registered trademarks of The Education Center, LLC. All other brand or product names are trademarks or registered trademarks of their respective companies.

Printed in the United States
10 9 8 7 6 5 4 3 2 1

HPS246110

Table of Contents

Thematic Units

Perfectly Pleasing Pumpkins! 3
Highlight this popular fall fruit with these kid-pleasing, skill-building pumpkin-themed ideas!

Plentiful Pumpkins! 8
This assortment of fun activities is geared to yield a bumper crop of learning opportunities.

In the Pumpkin Patch 14
Seeds of learning will no doubt sprout and grow with this selection of pumpkin-related activities!

Pumpkin Science 18
Little learners develop scientific process skills with these hands-on pumpkin investigations.

More Pumpkin Ideas 22
Build an assortment of developmentally appropriate skills with even more pumpkin-themed activities, center and group ideas, songs and rhymes, arts and crafts, classroom displays, and a snack recipe and cards.

"How a Pumpkin Grows" Booklet 39
This adorable booklet can be used to introduce or review the life cycle of a pumpkin.

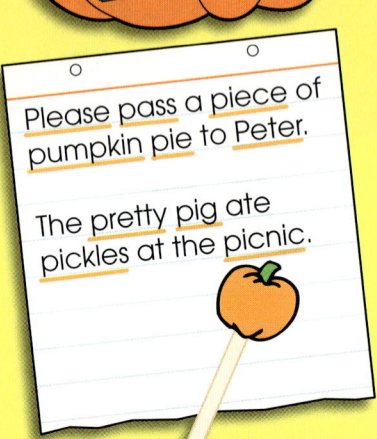

Reproducible Practice Pages 44
Reinforce literacy and math skills with these simple-to-use practice pages!

Perfectly Pleasing Pumpkins!

This divine collection of ideas celebrates that famous fall fruit—the pumpkin!

Pumpkin Positions
Positional words

This little mouse needs a nice big pumpkin to hide in! Cut out a copy of the mouse pattern on page 6. Also cut the top off a pumpkin and remove the insides. (As an alternative, use a pumpkin cutout and alter the activity accordingly.) Give a child the mouse and lead students in reciting the rhyme shown, prompting the student to move the mouse as indicated. Continue with different volunteers and positional words.

A tiny little mouse (squeak, squeak, squeak, squeak)
Walks up to a pumpkin (sneak, sneak, sneak, sneak).
He hides [beside] the pumpkin, and he shivers in fright
Because it's dark and spooky on Halloween night.

Continue with the following: *in, on, behind, in front of, under*

Give Me a *P!*
Matching and naming letters

Make a class supply of pumpkin cutouts (patterns on page 7). Write a letter from the word *pumpkin* on each cutout. Then write the word *pumpkin* on the board. Scatter the pumpkins around your room. Invite students to find one pumpkin each and then return to their seats. Point to the first *P* on the board and say, "Give me a *P!*" Prompt all youngsters with the letter *P* on their pumpkins to stand, hold up their pumpkins, and say, "*P!*" Continue with each remaining letter. Then say, "What does that spell?" and prompt students to answer, "Pumpkin!" If desired, hide the pumpkins again and play another round.

Marie E. Cecchini, West Dundee, IL

Plentiful Ps

Recognizing letter P

Cut out several copies of the letter cards on page 6. Place the cards at a center along with a pumpkin and tape. Have children visit the center and find the Ps. Then have them tape the Ps to the pumpkin.

Keely Saunders, Bonney Lake ECEAP, Bonney Lake, WA

Did You Ever?

Participating in a song

This fun little action song highlights pumpkin variety!

(sung to the tune of "Did You Ever See a Lassie?")

Did you ever see the pumpkins, The pumpkins, the pumpkins? Did you ever see the pumpkins That grow on the vine—	Hold arms in front as if holding a pumpkin and sway.
The fat ones and thin ones And tall ones and small ones? Did you ever see the pumpkins That grow on the vine?	Hold hands wide apart and then close together. Hold one hand above head and then close to floor. Repeat first action.

Marie E. Cecchini, West Dundee, IL

Plumply, Dumply

Sorting, reinforcing rhyming words

Cut out several copies of the pumpkin patterns on page 7 and place them in a bag. Make the headings shown for your pocket chart. Read aloud *Plumply, Dumply Pumpkin* by Mary Serfozo. In this story, Peter the tiger bypasses lumpy, bumpy pumpkins to find a perfect plumply, dumply pumpkin. Have a child choose a pumpkin from the bag. Have him hold up the pumpkin. Then encourage students to label the pumpkin by saying "Plumply, dumply!" or "Lumpy, bumpy!" Prompt the student to place the pumpkin in the chart appropriately. Continue with the remaining pumpkins. After the activity, give each child a plumply, dumply pumpkin cutout and have him decorate it to make a showy, glowy jack-o'-lantern!

Jack-o'-Lantern of Mine

Participating in a song

If desired, have each student transform a pumpkin pattern (see page 7) into a jack-o'-lantern stick puppet. Then have students wave their puppets in the air during the first verse and blow a quick puff of air on their puppets when indicated during the second verse. What terrific pumpkin fun!

(sung to the tune of "This Little Light of Mine")

Jack-o'-lantern of mine,
Watch you glow and shine.
Jack-o'-lantern of mine,
Watch you glow and shine.
Jack-o'-lantern of mine,
Watch you glow and shine,
Glow and shine, glow and shine, glow and shine!

Jack-o'-lantern of mine,
I'm going to blow you out. *(Puff!)*
Jack-o'-lantern of mine,
I'm going to blow you out. *(Puff!)*
Jack-o'-lantern of mine,
I'm going to blow you out,
Blow you out, blow you out, blow you out! *(Puff! Puff!)*

Roxanne LaBell Dearman, Western NC Early Intervention Program for Children Who Are Deaf or Hard of Hearing, Charlotte, NC

Print It!

Expressing oneself through art

To make this pumpkin project, dip the end of a cardboard tube into orange paint and then press the tube on a sheet of paper to make several prints (pumpkins). If desired, attach construction paper stems to the pumpkins. Then use a squeeze-style condiment container filled with diluted green paint to draw vines on the project.

Mary Ellen Moore, Miller Elementary, Canton, MI

Faux Pumpkin Fun!

Developing role-playing skills

With this activity, youngsters act out fun Halloween traditions! Cut a hole in the top of a faux pumpkin. Then cut a simple face in the pumpkin. Provide plastic knives, scoops, battery operated candles, newspapers, and white pieces of yarn mixed with craft foam seeds (pumpkin goop). Children can act out picking the pumpkin, placing it on newspapers, and carving it. They may even want to pick out the pumpkin seeds and pretend to roast them on a cookie sheet!

Donna Olp, St. Gregory the Great Preschool, South Euclid, OH

Mouse Pattern
Use with "Pumpkin Positions" on page 3.

Letter Cards
Use with "Plentiful Ps" on page 4.

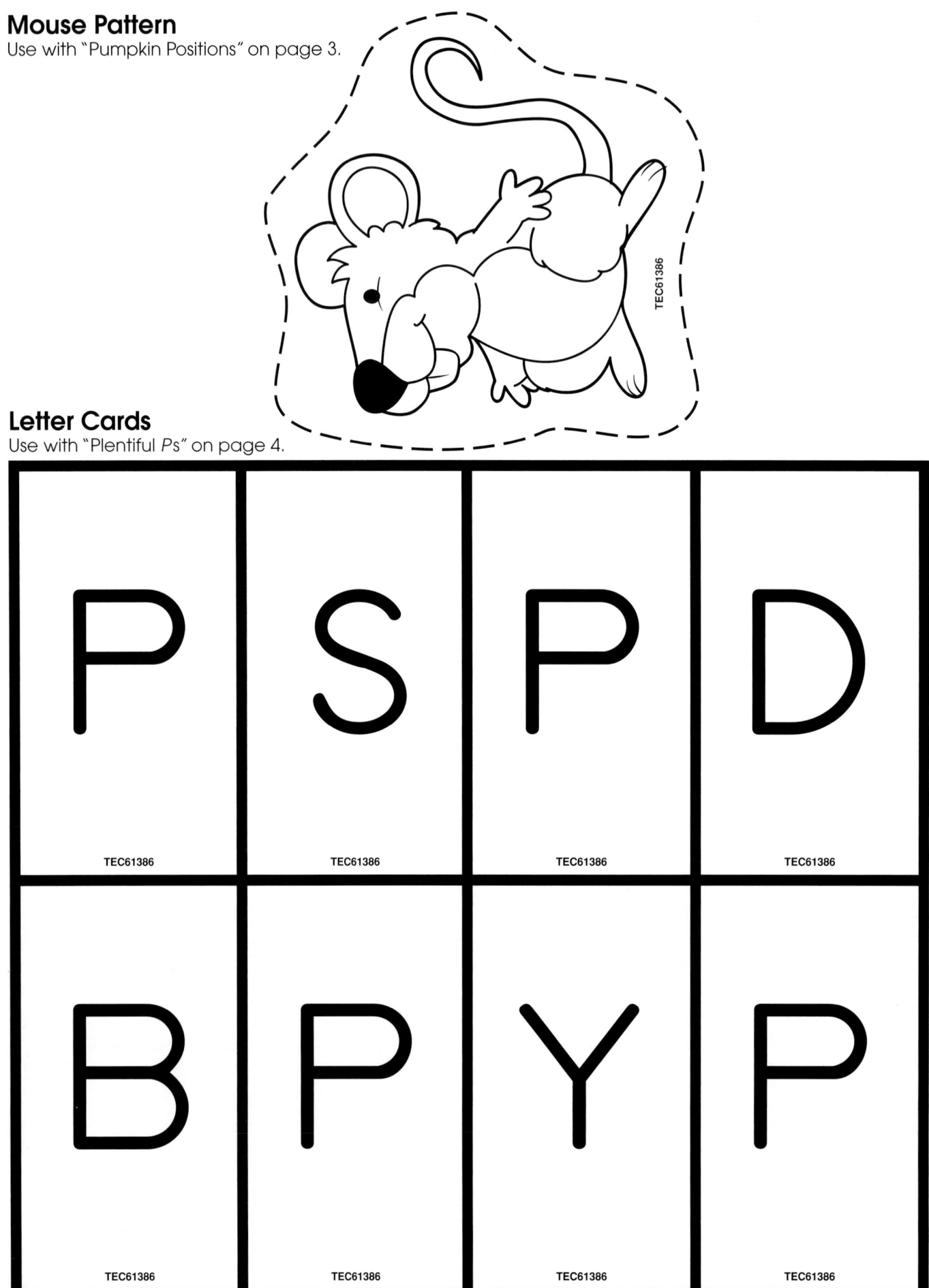

Pumpkin Patterns

Use with "Give Me a *P*!" on page 3, "Plumply, Dumply" on page 4, and "Jack-o'-Lantern of Mine" on page 5.

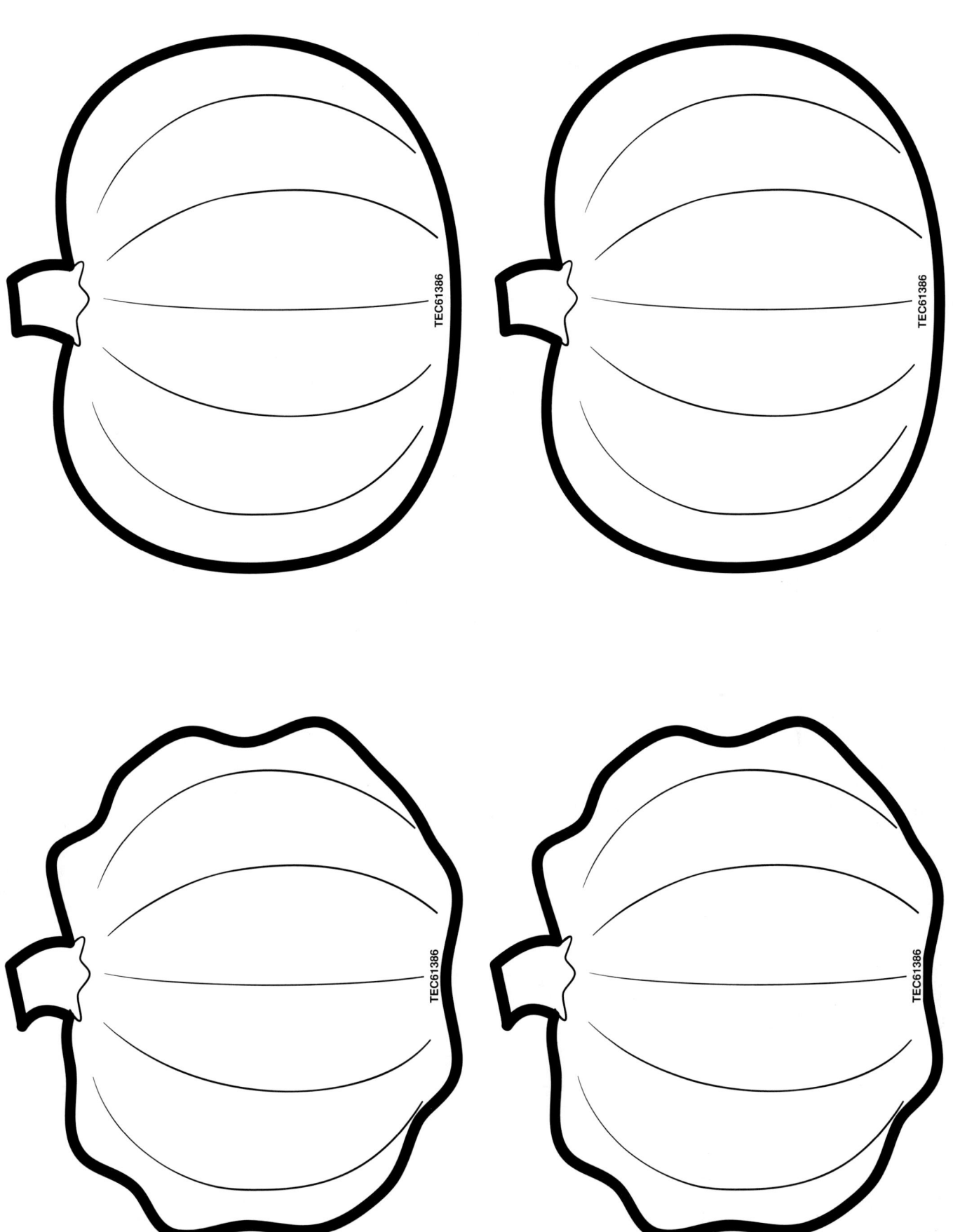

Plentiful Pumpkins!

Peruse this pumpkin patch and harvest a bumper crop of learning opportunities. No doubt the result will be oodles of cheery grins!

ideas contributed by Ada Goren, Winston-Salem, NC

What Is It?
Singing a song

Spotlight pumpkins with this divine little ditty! Make an orange pumpkin cutout for each child plus one for yourself. Place the pumpkin behind your back and sing to your youngsters the song shown, omitting the spoken line at the end. Have students guess the object that the song describes. When they guess that the item is a pumpkin, reveal the cutout. Next, give each child her own cutout and have her hide it behind her back. Then lead students in singing the song, having them add the final spoken line as they reveal their own hidden pumpkins!

Suzanne Moore, Irving, TX

(sung to the tune of "Six Little Ducks")

I'm very orange, and I am round.
I grew from a seed down in the ground.
You can carve me a face or put me in a pie.
Now take a guess and tell me,
What am I? What am I? What am I?
Now take a guess and tell me, what am I?

(spoken) A pumpkin!

In Line on the Vine
Ordering numerals

Make five orange construction paper copies of the pumpkin pattern on page 11. Label each pumpkin with a different numeral from 1 to 5 and the corresponding number of dots. Also label each of five index cards in the same manner. Tape to a flat surface a length of green yarn (vine) and green construction paper leaves. Then tape the index cards in order along the vine. Place the prepared pumpkins nearby. A child puts the matching pumpkin on top of each index card to arrange the pumpkins from 1 to 5. For more advanced students, omit the index cards from the activity.

Orange, Round, and Gooey!
Using descriptive words

For each child, staple two orange construction paper pumpkins together (see the pattern on page 11). Personalize the top pumpkin in each set. To begin, display a pumpkin that has the top removed. Have students touch and describe the outside and then the inside of the pumpkin as you write their words on a sheet of chart paper. Next, give each child his prepared pumpkin cutouts. Have him glue pieces of yellow yarn and cleaned and dried pumpkin seeds to the bottom cutout so it resembles the inside of the pumpkin. When the glue is dry, display the projects and the chart paper in your classroom.

Hilarie Hutt, Summit School, Summit, SD

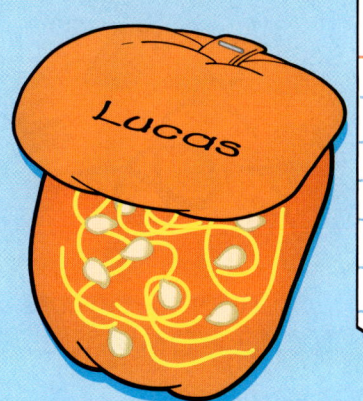

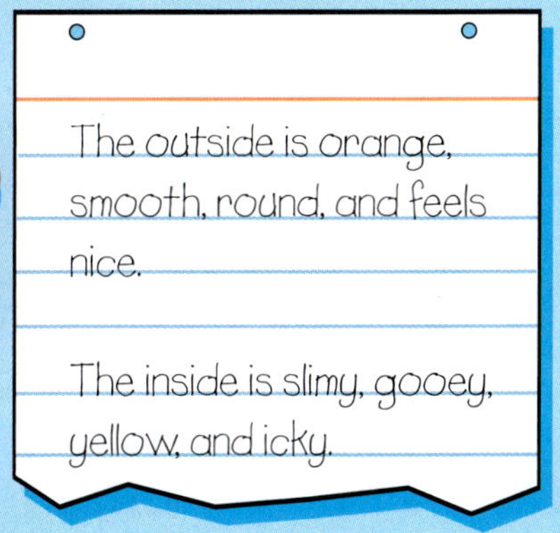

The outside is orange, smooth, round, and feels nice.

The inside is slimy, gooey, yellow, and icky.

Flannelboard Faces
Matching shapes

Youngsters transform a plain pumpkin into a jazzy jack-o'-lantern at this flannelboard center! Color and cut out a copy of the jack-o'-lantern cards on page 12. Then laminate them for durability. Cut from felt a large orange pumpkin and the following black shapes: three triangles, three circles, three squares, and a rectangle. Place the pumpkin on your flannelboard. Then set the cards and shapes nearby. A child chooses a card and then places shapes on the pumpkin to duplicate the face shown. After admiring her pumpkin, she removes the shapes. Then she continues in the same way with each remaining card.

A Prizewinning Patch
Developing fine-motor skills

Youngsters create a pleasing pumpkin patch mural with prints made from miniature pumpkins! Tape a length of bulletin board paper to a table. Cut a miniature pumpkin in half and place the halves, cut side down, in a shallow pan of orange tempera paint. Place the pan at the table. Next, invite one or two youngsters to the table and encourage them to make several prints on the paper. Repeat the process until each child in the room has had an opportunity to make prints. When the paint is dry, invite students to cut green construction paper leaves and then glue them to the paper. Embellish the patch with green curling ribbon (vines). Then post this nifty mural on a wall in your classroom!

Pass the Pumpkin
Listening for beginning sound /p/

Harvest phonemic awareness skills with this circle-time idea! Cut out a copy of the picture cards on page 13; then place them in a plastic trick-or-treat pumpkin. Gather students in a circle. Have youngsters pass the pumpkin around the circle as you lead them in singing the song shown. When the song is finished, locate the child holding the pumpkin and encourage him to remove a card. Have the student name the picture. Then instruct all the youngsters to say the name of the picture, emphasizing the /p/ sound at the beginning of the name. Continue in the same way for each card in the pumpkin.

(sung to the tune of "Clementine")

Pass the pumpkin, pass the pumpkin,
Pass the pumpkin round to me.
When it stops, I'll take out something
That begins with letter *P*!

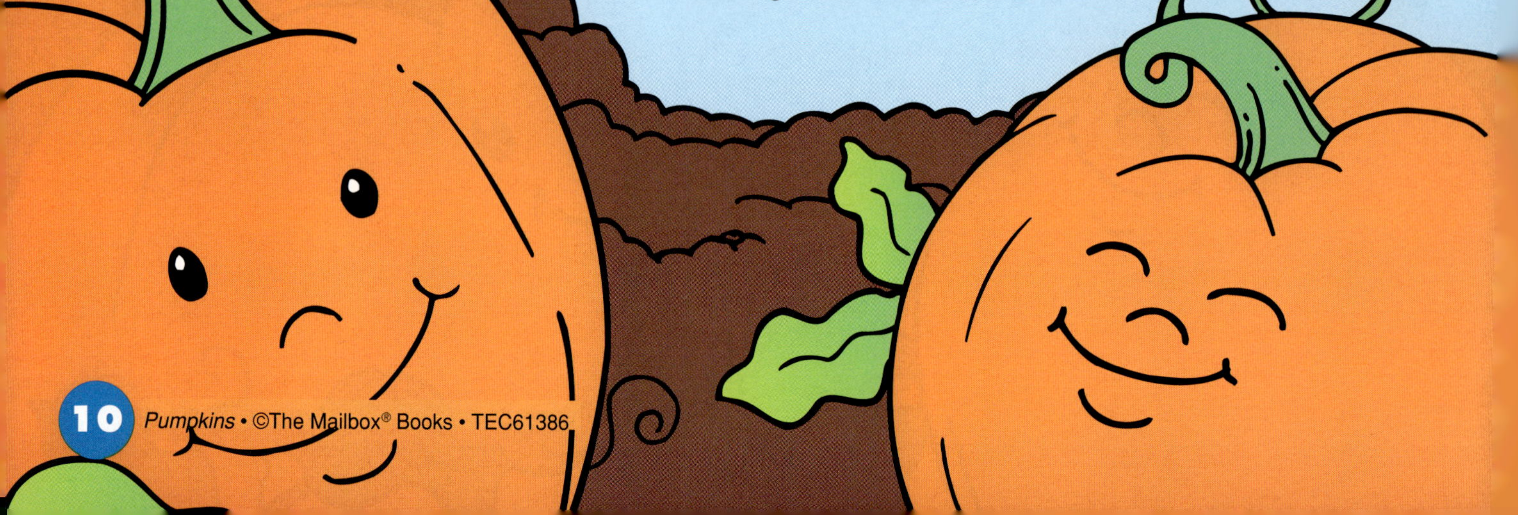

Pumpkin Pattern

Use with "In Line on the Vine" on page 8 and "Orange, Round, and Gooey!" on page 9.

Jack-o'-Lantern Cards
Use with "Flannelboard Faces" on page 9.

Picture Cards
Use with "Pass the Pumpkin" on page 10.

In the Pumpkin Patch

Use these fresh ideas to cultivate a variety of skills!

ideas by Laurie Gibbons
Huntsville, AL

Like an Orange?
Comparing and contrasting

Begin a class discussion about pumpkins with the help of a familiar fruit! Bring in an orange and a small pumpkin. If desired, bring in a few extra oranges and later cut them into wedges for student snacks. On a large sheet of paper, draw a pumpkin and an orange, as shown, and then add the section titles. Display the resulting poster.

To begin, have the youngsters observe details about the real pumpkin and orange, such as how they look and feel. Then guide students to use their observations and prior knowledge to compare and contrast the pumpkin and orange. Write each comment in the appropriate section of the poster. Keep the poster on display for several days to promote more thoughtful comparisons!

Pumpkin: heavy, stem, hard shell, smooth, grows on a vine
Both: orange, round, seeds, can be eaten
Orange: not heavy, small, smells good, grows on a tree

Pass the Words!
Using complete sentences

Use this group activity to harvest improved speaking and writing skills. Program each of several construction paper pumpkin seeds with a different pumpkin-related or fall word. Place the seeds in a plastic pumpkin container. To begin, hold the pumpkin as you sit with students in a circle. Then remove a seed, read it aloud, and have a volunteer use it in a complete sentence. Next, lead the students in repeating the sentence as they pass the pumpkin, saying one word each time the pumpkin is passed. The student who has the pumpkin when the last word is said sets it on the floor, removes a seed, and reads it aloud. After a volunteer uses the word in a sentence, the students repeat the sentence and pass the pumpkin as before. The activity continues in this manner until the pumpkin is empty.

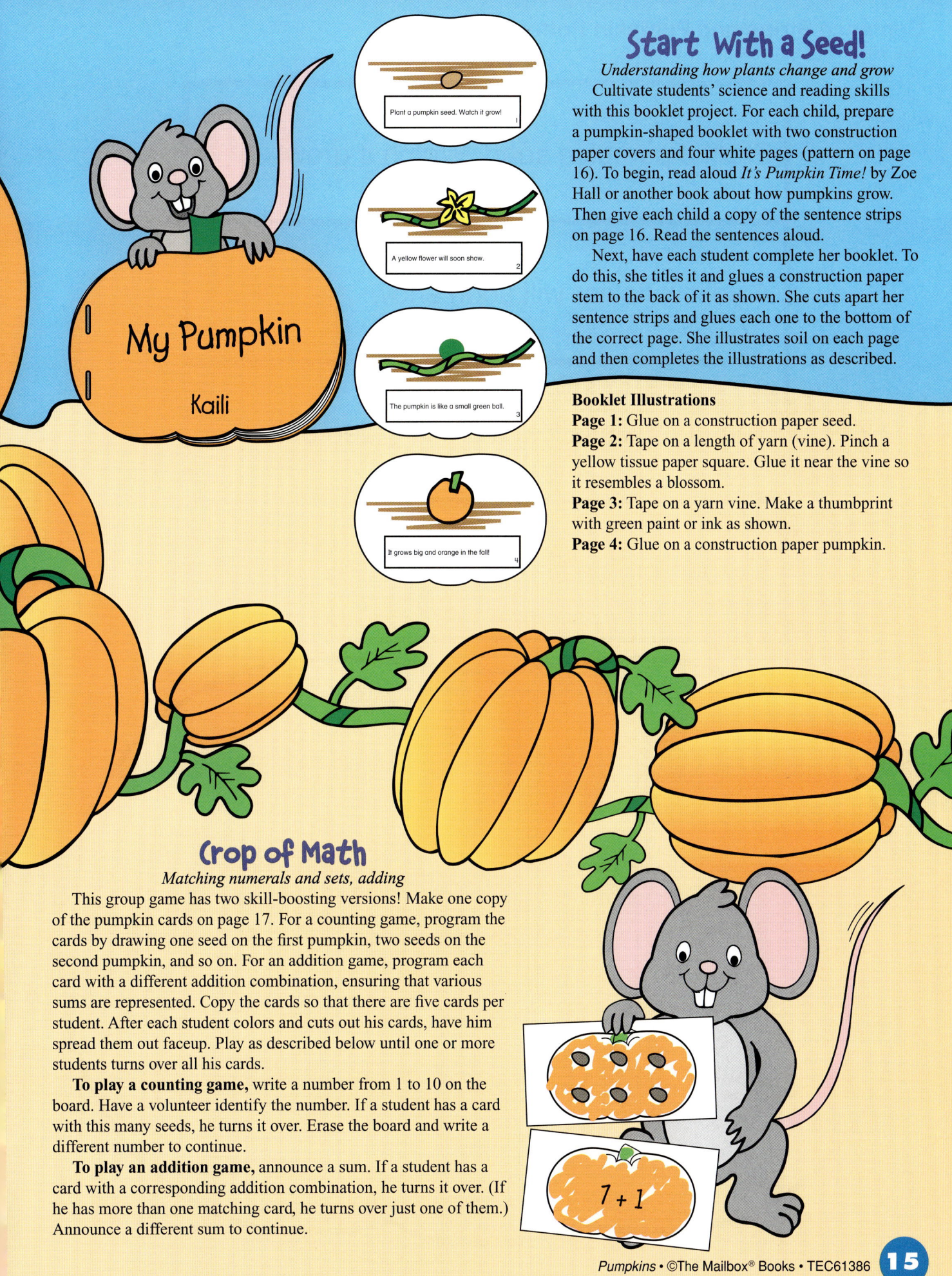

Start With a Seed!
Understanding how plants change and grow

Cultivate students' science and reading skills with this booklet project. For each child, prepare a pumpkin-shaped booklet with two construction paper covers and four white pages (pattern on page 16). To begin, read aloud *It's Pumpkin Time!* by Zoe Hall or another book about how pumpkins grow. Then give each child a copy of the sentence strips on page 16. Read the sentences aloud.

Next, have each student complete her booklet. To do this, she titles it and glues a construction paper stem to the back of it as shown. She cuts apart her sentence strips and glues each one to the bottom of the correct page. She illustrates soil on each page and then completes the illustrations as described.

Booklet Illustrations
Page 1: Glue on a construction paper seed.
Page 2: Tape on a length of yarn (vine). Pinch a yellow tissue paper square. Glue it near the vine so it resembles a blossom.
Page 3: Tape on a yarn vine. Make a thumbprint with green paint or ink as shown.
Page 4: Glue on a construction paper pumpkin.

Crop of Math
Matching numerals and sets, adding

This group game has two skill-boosting versions! Make one copy of the pumpkin cards on page 17. For a counting game, program the cards by drawing one seed on the first pumpkin, two seeds on the second pumpkin, and so on. For an addition game, program each card with a different addition combination, ensuring that various sums are represented. Copy the cards so that there are five cards per student. After each student colors and cuts out his cards, have him spread them out faceup. Play as described below until one or more students turns over all his cards.

To play a counting game, write a number from 1 to 10 on the board. Have a volunteer identify the number. If a student has a card with this many seeds, he turns it over. Erase the board and write a different number to continue.

To play an addition game, announce a sum. If a student has a card with a corresponding addition combination, he turns it over. (If he has more than one matching card, he turns over just one of them.) Announce a different sum to continue.

Sentence Strips and Pumpkin Pattern
Use with "Start With a Seed!" on page 15.

Plant a pumpkin seed. Watch it grow!	1
A yellow flower will soon show.	2
The pumpkin is like a small green ball.	3
It grows big and orange in the fall!	4

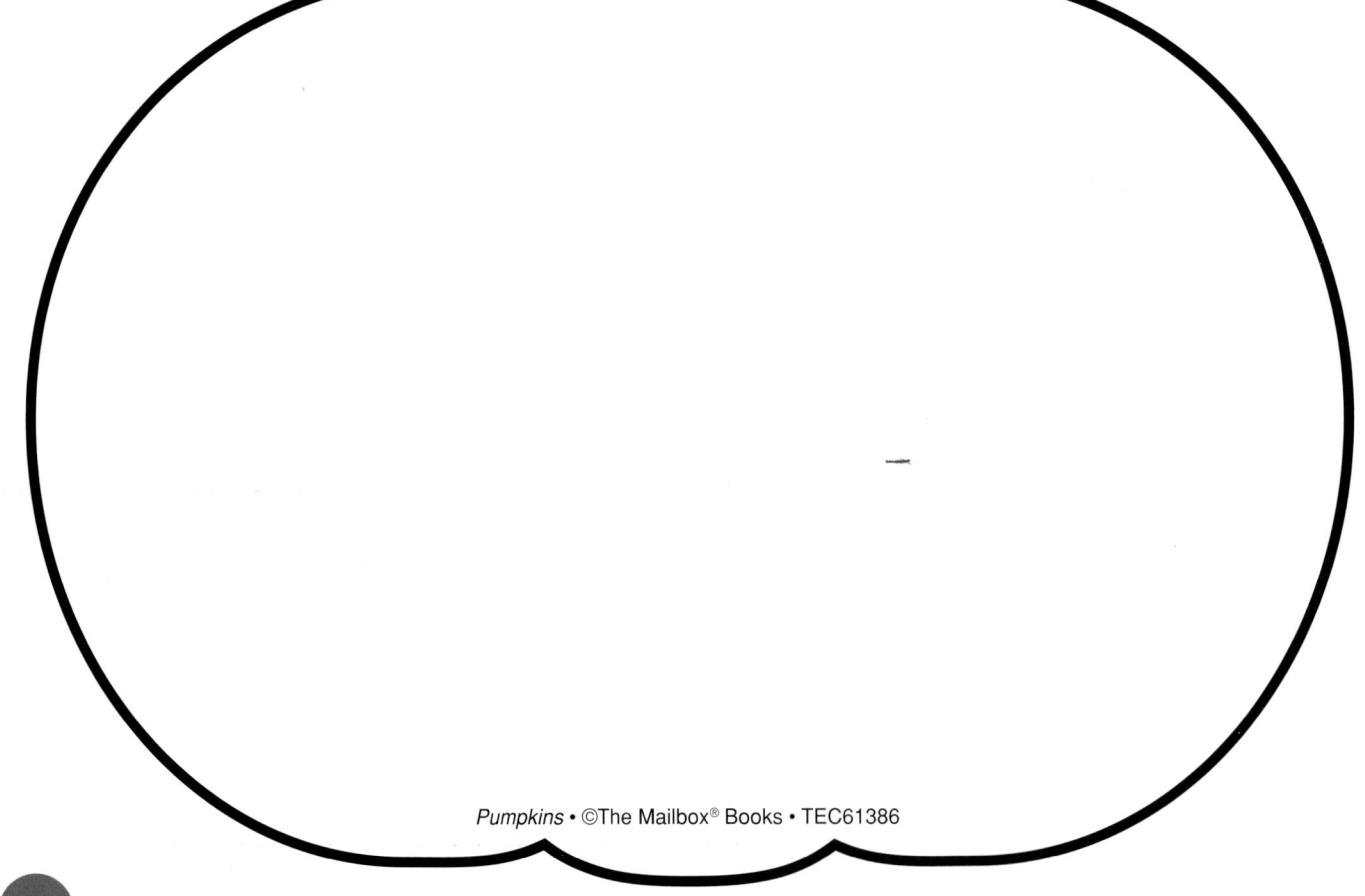

Pumpkin Cards
Use with "Crop of Math" on page 15.

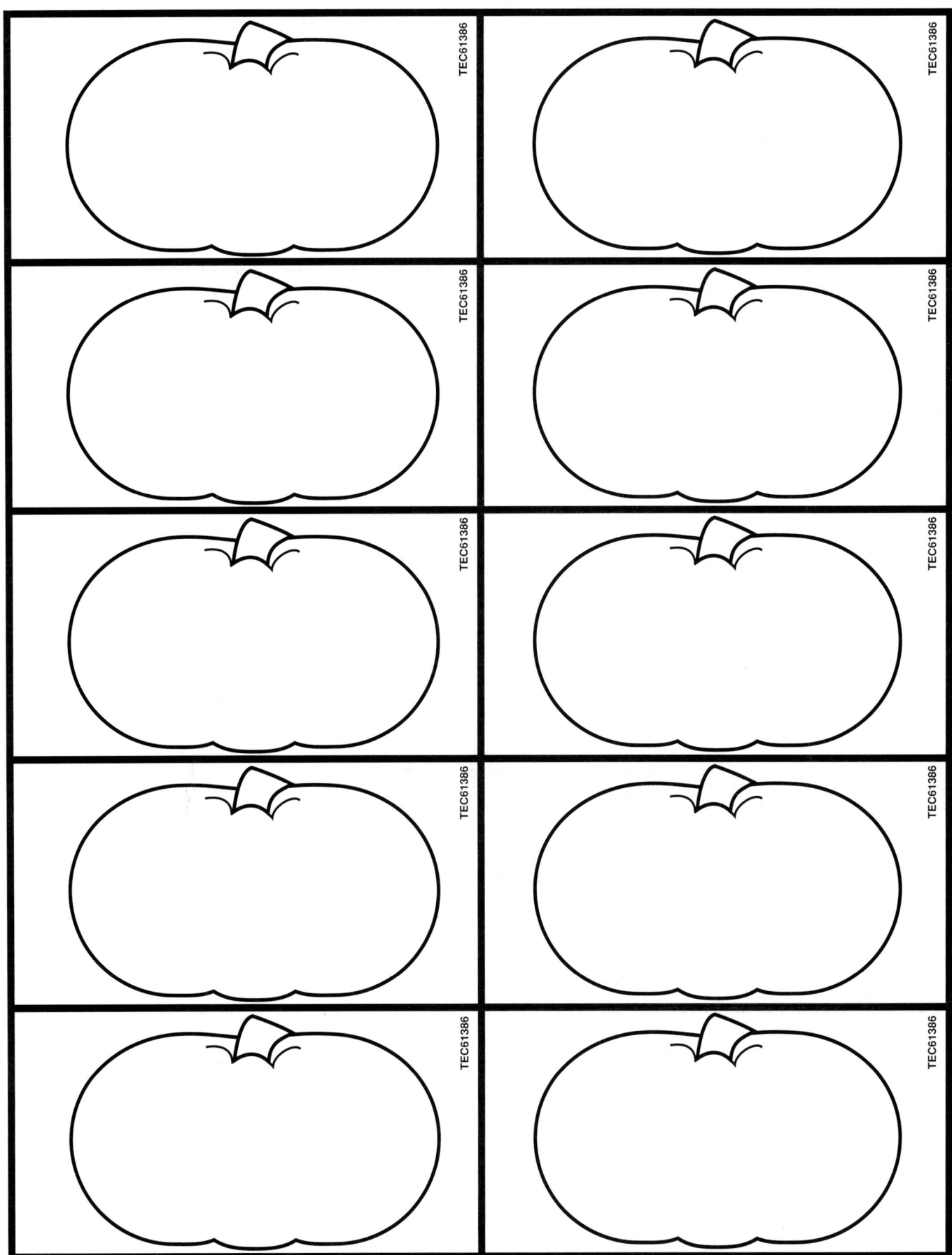

Pumpkin Science

Pokin' around the pumpkin patch we found lots of activities to develop youngsters' science process skills. It's time for your little scientists to ponder the properties of pumpkins. Let the investigations begin!

by Lucia Kemp Henry
Fallon, NV

Inferring

Undercover Pumpkin

Challenge your little ones to think like scientists with this guessing game. While students are out of the room, drape a cloth over a pumpkin so that it covers the pumpkin but still shows its size and shape. During a group time, use the riddle in the speech bubble to prompt the class to guess the identity of the hidden pumpkin. Your curious kiddies will become science sleuths quicker than you can say "jack-o'-lantern!"

> Here is something you can't see. Listen to these clues to guess what it might be.
> It grows from a seed, but it isn't a weed.
> It has a stem. It sits on the ground. Its shape is kind of round.
> Its color is orange like a tangerine. It smiles at you on Halloween.

Observing

Pumpkin Perceptions

Once your students have identified the seasonal subject to be studied, lead them in using their observation skills to learn more about the pumpkin. Have your group sit in a circle on the floor around the pumpkin. In turn, invite pairs of children to sit by the pumpkin so that they can touch it, smell it, and look at it closely. Encourage the children to communicate their observations by sharing words that describe the size, shape, color, and texture of the pumpkin. Record the descriptive words used on separate cards and attach the cards to the pumpkin.

Observing

The Inside Scoop

After students have examined the outsides of pumpkins, it's time to explore what's inside a pumpkin! To prepare, cover a table with newspaper or a vinyl tablecloth; then set a large pumpkin on the table. Invite students to describe the outside of the pumpkin; then ask each child to share what he thinks the *inside* of the pumpkin is like. Next, cut the top off the pumpkin so that students can inspect the inside and make some discoveries. Prompt hands-on observations by asking some questions such as the following:

What does the inside of the pumpkin look like?
What does it smell like?
What does it feel like?
How is the inside different from the outside of the pumpkin?

Invite each child, in turn, to help spoon out the seeds and the inside of the pumpkin. Discard the seeds and save the rest of the pumpkin to use in "Pumpkin Squish Test" to the right.

Observing
Comparing

Pumpkin Squish Test

Use this discovery center activity to squeeze some more science out of the humble pumpkin! To prepare, cut the pumpkin shell from "The Inside Scoop" into chunks. Simmer half of the chunks until the pulp is soft. Put the cooked and uncooked chunks in an empty sensory tub. Invite youngsters to discover which chunks of pumpkin are squishable and which ones aren't! Then help them describe how the chunks look and feel different.

How Does a Pumpkin Grow?

Your science-focused pumpkin study wouldn't be complete without reading a book about how pumpkins grow. Share and discuss *Pumpkin Pumpkin* by Jeanne Titherington. Then wrap up your unit with a song to help your little ones communicate what they've learned.

(sung to the tune of "How Much Is That Doggie in the Window?")

Oh, how does a pumpkin in the patch grow? It starts with a wee tiny seed.
You plant the seed in some really good soil. Yes, that's what the pumpkin will need.

Oh, how does a pumpkin in the patch grow? It starts with a wee tiny seed.
Then you need to give the seed some water. Yes, that's what the pumpkin will need.

Oh, how does a pumpkin in the patch grow? It starts with a wee tiny seed.
The seed will need a lot of sunshine. Yes, that's what the pumpkin will need.

Measuring
Recording Information

Personalized Pumpkin Study

This up close study of pint-sized pumpkins really measures up! In advance, collect a mini-pumpkin for each child; then use a permanent marker to write each child's name on the bottom of his pumpkin. Next, duplicate page 21 to create a class supply. Cut each page apart on the bold lines. To prepare a pumpkin report folder for each child, fold a 12" x 18" piece of orange construction paper in half. Glue the section titled "My Pumpkin Report" to the front of the folder and then glue the remaining sections to the inside of the folder as shown. Once each child's folder is assembled, follow the suggestions below to help each child measure and record his pumpkin data.

Pumpkin Report Cover
Have each child write his name on the cover. Encourage each child to draw and color a picture of his pumpkin; then have him cut it out and glue it onto the cover. Or take a photo of the child holding his pumpkin and glue the developed photo to the cover.

Circumference
Assist each child in measuring around his pumpkin with a piece of yarn. Help the child glue his yarn to the inside left page of the pumpkin report, leaving the folder open until the glue is dry.

Weight
Help each child weigh his pumpkin on a balance scale. Have him count the weights used to balance the scale; then have him place one dot sticker for each weight in the appropriate box inside his folder.

Height
Provide each child with a one-inch-wide strip of construction paper. Help him hold the strip upright next to his pumpkin and then make a pencil mark on the strip to show the pumpkin's height. Have him cut the strip off at the mark and then glue it to the appropriate section of the folder.

My Pumpkin Report

by _____

Pumpkins • ©The Mailbox® Books • TEC61386

My pumpkin is this **fat**.

My pumpkin **weighs** this much.

My pumpkin is this **tall**.

More Pumpkin

The Letter Patch
Letter recognition

Program pumpkin cutouts with different letters. Have youngsters stand in a circle; then place a pumpkin on the floor in front of each child. Lead students in the song shown as youngsters walk around the circle of pumpkins. When the song ends, have each student stop in front of a pumpkin. Name a letter and prompt the children with matching letters to hold the pumpkins in the air. After confirming that each letter is correct, youngsters place the pumpkins back on the floor.

(sung to the tune of "Pawpaw Patch")

Where, oh, where can we find letters?
Where, oh, where can we find letters?
Where, oh, where can we find letters?
Way down yonder in the pumpkin patch!

Mary Robles, Portland, OR

Pick a Letter
Letter identification

For this partner activity, make two pumpkin gameboards like the one shown. Set out the gameboards and a plastic pumpkin-shaped pail containing two sets of letter manipulatives. To take a turn, a child removes a letter from the pail and names it. Then he places the letter on his gameboard. If he chooses a letter that is covered, he returns the letter to the pail and his turn is over. Play continues until all the letters on both gameboards are covered. To reinforce uppercase-lowercase letter matching, write lowercase letters on the gameboards and put uppercase letters in the pail.

Leonor Maya
George Washington School
Schiller Park, IL

Ideas

In the Pumpkin Patch
Syllables

Counting syllables helps this pumpkin patch grow! To prepare for this center, program a large sheet of green paper (pumpkin patch) as shown. Place the pumpkin patch at a center along with a cut-out copy of the cards from page 36. For each card, a child names the picture, quietly claps once for each syllable, and then places the card in the matching row.

Kathryn Davenport, Partin Elementary, Oviedo, FL

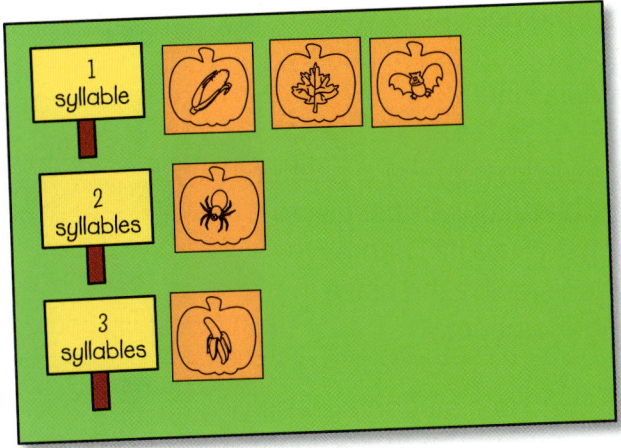

Pumpkin Punctuation
Using a period

After a visit to a pumpkin patch or after having a pumpkin-carving experience, save some pumpkin seeds for this display of pumpkin punctuation! Cut a large pumpkin shape from orange and green bulletin board paper and mount it on a wall. Have each child tell something about the class experience. Record each child's response as a complete sentence on the pumpkin. Then invite her to glue a dried pumpkin seed at the end of her sentence to represent the period. After everyone has contributed, you'll have a fine display about pumpkins…period!

Lin Attaya
Hodge Elementary
Denton, TX

Fall Favorite

Write the poem shown on strips for pocket chart use. Then try these activities!

Print awareness: For a pointer, glue one end of a craft stick to a pumpkin cutout. Then have individuals guide the class in reciting the poem.

Rhyming: Help students identify rhyming word pairs in the poem.

High-frequency words: Write high-frequency words from the poem on pumpkin cutouts. Slide the cutouts in front of the matching words. Have students take turns picking pumpkins. To pick one, a child reads the word and then drops the cutout in a basket.

Ada Goren, Winston-Salem, NC

Pumpkins, pumpkins on a vine.
Pumpkins, pumpkins look so fine!
I like pumpkins; yes, I do!
Big and orange for me and you!

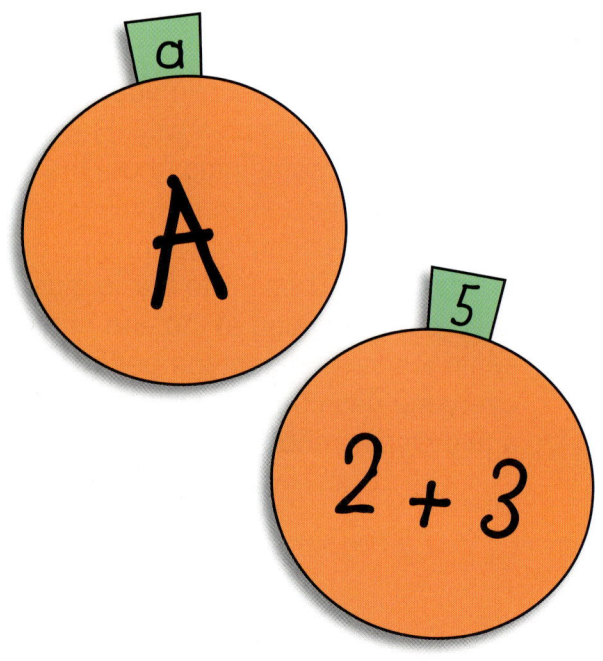

Where's My Stem?
Skill practice

Use this whole-group game to practice a variety of skills! Cut out orange circles (pumpkins) for half your students and the same number of green rectangles (stems). Label the pumpkin and stem pairs to practice a skill, such as uppercase and lowercase letters, addition facts and answers, or color dots and color words. Then give each child a cutout. To play, youngsters work together to correctly pair each pumpkin with its stem. **For an independent activity,** place the prepared pumpkins and stems at a center.

Laurie Gibbons, Huntsville, AL

Pumpkin, Pumpkin, What Do You See?

Vocabulary, color words

Teach your youngsters this familiar book refrain with a pumpkin twist to promote language skills. In advance, cut two eyeholes in a nine-inch paper plate and then paint the plate orange to create a pumpkin mask. When the paint is dry, glue a green construction paper stem and a large craft stick handle to the back of the mask.

During a circle time, discuss the different plants that grow in a garden and then record students' answers on a chart. Give the mask to one child and ask her to pretend she is a pumpkin looking around her garden to see what is growing nearby. Have the class recite the first line of the chant to the right. Ask the pumpkin to respond by chanting the second line, substituting a color word and a plant name, such as *yellow squash*, *red tomato*, *orange carrot*, or *tan cantaloupe*. Repeat the activity until each child has had a turn.

Pumpkin, pumpkin, what do you see?
I see a [green cucumber] growing near me!

Heavier or Lighter?

Making comparisons, writing

A pumpkin is the only prop needed for these weighty comparisons! Display a medium-size pumpkin. Post a chart with two columns, one labeled "Heavier" and the other labeled "Lighter." Then have students name items that are heavier or lighter than the pumpkin. List each item in the correct column. Next, each youngster draws a line down the center of a sheet of paper. On one side of the line, she illustrates something that is lighter than the pumpkin. On the other side, she shows something that is heavier than the pumpkin. She adds captions and then shares her comparison with a classmate.

Lin Attaya, Hodge Elementary, Denton, TX

Toothy Grins
Counting, making and comparing sets

Youngsters practice counting to give these jack-o'-lanterns great big toothy grins! Enlarge the pumpkin pattern on page 37; then make two orange construction paper copies. Cut facial features from each pumpkin, omitting the teeth; then color the stems green and mount the pumpkins on yellow construction paper. Place the resulting jack-o'-lanterns at a table along with a jumbo die and orange paper squares (teeth). Two youngsters visit the center. One child rolls the die and places the corresponding number of teeth on a pumpkin. His partner repeats the process with the second pumpkin. Then the children compare the pumpkins, using words such as *more*, *less*, or *same*.

Leslie Seabase, Saginaw Chippewa Academy, Mt. Pleasant, MI

Top the Pies
Number identification, making sets

Decorate five orange paper circles so they resemble pumpkin pies. Program each pie with a different number and add a matching dot set to the back, if desired. Provide a supply of cotton balls (dollops of whipped cream). If desired, place the cotton balls in a clean whipped-cream container. A youngster chooses a pie and identifies the number. Then she places that number of whipped-cream dollops on the pie.

Henry Fergus
Phoenix, AZ

Pumpkin Poll
Counting tally marks, comparing numbers

Here's a fresh way to introduce your students to the idea of an election. Display a pumpkin and tell students that they will vote on the following day to determine what type of face to give it. Present the choices and prompt discussion to build anticipation. On the election day, have each youngster complete a ballot similar to the one shown and then deposit it in a decorated box. After all the votes are cast, ceremoniously remove the ballots one by one, and use tally marks to record the votes on the board. Ask students to determine the totals and compare the numbers to identify the winning choice. Then serve cider or another seasonal treat as you decorate the pumpkin!

Ada Goren
Winston-Salem, NC

Geometric Jacks
Shape recognition

These jack-o'-lanterns treat students to lots of practice with shapes! To prepare, cut several different large pumpkins from orange felt. Then cut out felt accessories (such as hats and bows), leaves, and black felt facial features in a variety of shapes. Store all the felt pieces in a plastic trick-or-treat bucket. Have students work in pairs to create unique pumpkin faces. Instruct one child to create a face and then describe it to his partner. Can she make an identical face on her pumpkin without peeking at his design?

Karen Coldiron
First Kids Preschool and Kindergarten
Somerset, KY

Pumpkin Stack
Using nonstandard measurement

Make several orange construction paper copies of the pumpkin pattern on page 37. Attach the pumpkins to a wall so they appear to be stacked one on top of the other. Take a photo of each child standing next to the pumpkin stack. Then attach each photo to a sheet of construction paper programmed as shown. Encourage the child to count how many pumpkins tall she is. Then help her write the number on her paper. Bind the finished pages and a cover together to make a book titled "How Many Pumpkins Tall?" Then place the finished class book in your reading center.

Amy Ryan, Grace Lutheran School, St. Petersburg, FL

Pumpkin Exploration
Using standard measurement

After a visit to the pumpkin patch, have each child record descriptive information about his pumpkin in this unique booklet. Follow the steps below to make one booklet for each child. Then place the booklets at a center along with a measuring tape, a scale, and some crayons. Invite each of your youngsters to bring his pumpkin to the center and help him complete his booklet.

To make one booklet:
1. Paint two paper plates orange and then set them aside to dry. (Or use orange party plates.)
2. Program four white paper plates as shown and then stack them between the two orange plates.
3. Punch two holes through the top of the plates; then place a metal ring through each hole to bind the plates together.
4. Glue a brown construction paper stem to the front cover of the booklet.
5. Glue a photograph of the child with his pumpkin to the inside of the back cover.

Krista Crates Miller, Findlay, OH

Pumpkin Prints
Art

You'll make authentic pumpkin prints with this crafty idea! After carving your classroom jack-o'-lantern, remove any excess pulp from the facial cutouts; then wash and dry the pieces. Simply dip one of the features in paint and then press it onto an orange construction paper pumpkin cutout. Continue in the same way with the remaining pumpkin parts to create your own unique jack-o'-lantern.

Heather E. Graley
Grace Christian School
Blacklick, OH

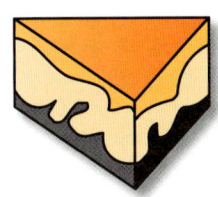

Perfect Pumpkins
Art

These pumpkins are *cute!* Give each child a small foam ball that has been flattened on one side by pressing it against a table. Have her glue pieces of orange tissue paper all over the ball, being sure to overlap the pieces. When the glue is dry, help the child stick a two-inch piece of green pipe cleaner into the top of her pumpkin to create a stem. Then, if desired, have her draw eyes, a nose, and a mouth on her pumpkin with a black marker. Display these pumpkins for everyone to admire!

Stacy Beman
Plaza Boulevard Child Development Center
Rapid City, SD

Chalk and Water Art
Process art

Here's an anytime art experience your youngsters will love! First, fill a sink or large container with water. Have each child use a handheld pencil sharpener to sharpen sticks of colorful chalk, dropping the chalkdust into the water. Do *not* mix the chalk into the water—allow the chalkdust to float. You'll be able to see a swirling design form. Next, have a child lay a white construction paper pumpkin on top of the water and press down very gently. Have him lift the paper off the water's surface and lay it design-side up to dry. Can he see the swirl design on his paper? Cool!

Debbie Rowland, Seoul, Korea

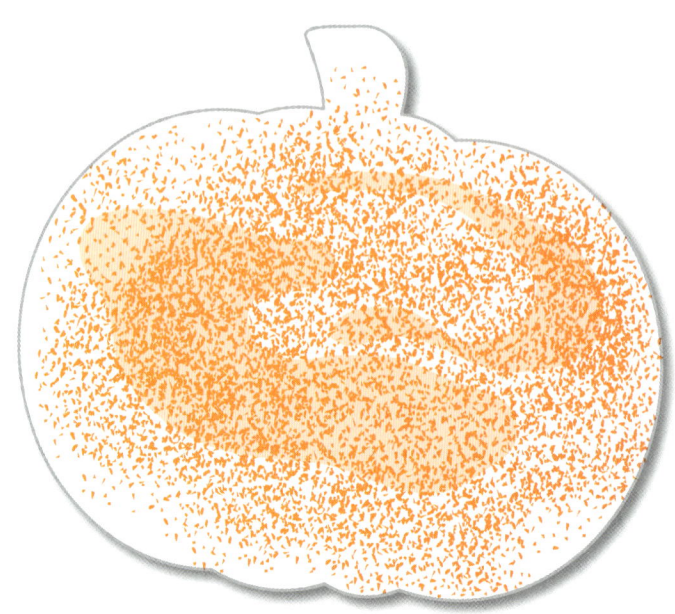

Plump Pumpkins
Art

Create an eye-catching autumn display with a patch of these three-dimensional pumpkins! To make a pumpkin, trace a pattern similar to the one shown on a 9" x 12" sheet of orange construction paper. After you cut out the tracing, draw lines so they resemble the lines on a pumpkin shell. Next, loosely curl a length of green curling ribbon and then tape it near the top of the pumpkin. Glue on a construction paper stem, concealing the taped end of the curling ribbon. If desired, decorate the pumpkin with construction paper eyes, a nose, and a mouth. To complete the pumpkin, cut four diagonal lines as shown. Then overlap the paper slightly at each cut and secure it on the back of the project with masking tape.

Donna L. Browning
Northampton Elementary
Spring, TX

Big Orange Pumpkins

This little ditty takes pumpkins from seeds to festive jack-o'-lanterns!

(sung to the tune of "The Itsy-Bitsy Spider")

Pumpkins start as fat seeds
Planted in the ground.
Then they push up vines
That wiggle all around.
Soon pumpkins grow.
They're big and orange too.
Then you carve a jack-o'-lantern
That lights up and says, "Boo!"

Deborah Garmon
Groton, CT

Pumpkin Trees?

This giggle-inducing action rhyme is sure to become a classroom favorite! Lead students in reciting the rhyme, pausing briefly after the question in the fourth line for youngsters to share their responses.

It's harvesttime, and what do I see? *Put hand up to forehead. Look around.*
Pumpkins! Pumpkins in a tree! *Point upward.*
In a tree? That can't be! *Place hands on cheeks.*
Where, oh where, should pumpkins be? *Throw hands outward.*
On the ground? Yes, on the ground! *Point to the ground.*
That's where pumpkins should be found! *Place hands on hips.*

Deirdre Banks
Growing Angels Center for Learning
Fort Meade, MD

Pick of the Crop

Your students are sure to enjoy this toe-tapping ditty about one large, ripe pumpkin!

(sung to the tune of "Three Blind Mice")

One big pumpkin,
One big pumpkin.
Round and orange,
Round and orange.
We found it and picked it from our crop.
We brought it inside and cut off the top.
We carved a face and took out the slop.
Now it's one silly pumpkin.

Julie Granchelli
Lockport, NY

Pick a Pumpkin

It's pumpkin-pickin' time! Get your youngsters in the mood by singing this little ditty!

(sung to the tune of "London Bridge")

Pick a pumpkin from the vine,
Pumpkin round, pumpkin fine.
Pick a pumpkin from the vine.
Let's pick pumpkins!

Pick a pumpkin from the vine.
You pick yours; I'll pick mine.
Pick a pumpkin from the vine.
Let's pick pumpkins!

Betty Silkunas
Lower Gwynedd Elementary
Ambler, PA

A pumpkin patch takes shape when youngsters make this bulletin board. Have each child mix red and yellow paint on an old cookie sheet to make a thin layer of orange. Then help her press a large pumpkin-shaped white paper cutout in the paint to make a print. When dry, write each child's name on her pumpkin. Attach the pumpkins to a board and add the title shown.

Nancy O'Toole, Ready Set Grow, Grand Rapids, MN

After a student listens to a read-aloud, help him complete an orange copy of the book report form from page 38 and have him color the pumpkin stem. Display youngsters' completed forms with leaf cutouts and crepe paper streamers (vines) as desired.

Darlene Martin, South Elementary, Hingham, MA

Classroom Café

Use the recipe below to help your students prepare yummy pumpkin look-alikes. Then highlight the letter *p* with the sentence-stretching activity that follows!

Pair of Pumpkins

Ingredients for one:
2 tsp. whipped topping
1 tsp. pumpkin pie filling
2 vanilla wafers
2 pretzel rod pieces (stems)

Utensils and supplies:
disposable cup for each student
2 measuring teaspoons
small paper plate for each student
plastic spoons
plastic knives

Teacher preparation:
- Arrange the supplies and ingredients for easy student access.
- Post a copy of the recipe (page 35) as desired. Or give each student a copy; then ask her to cut apart the cards and staple them to make a booklet.

adapted from an idea by Judi Lesnansky
New Hope Academy
Youngstown, OH

Please pass a piece of pumpkin pie to Peter.

The pretty pig ate pickles at the picnic.

After the Recipe

P is for *pumpkin, patch,* and plenty of other pleasing words! As students enjoy the snacks that they prepared, point out that the words *pair* and *pumpkins* have the same beginning letter. Post a jumbo letter *P* that you have cut from white paper. Have students name words that begin with *p;* write them on the displayed letter. Next, say a sentence with two of the words. Guide students to revise the sentence to include more *p* words; write the revision on a sheet of chart paper. Then have volunteers underline the *p* words with an orange marker. After you prepare a few more alliterative sentences in this manner, invite students to practice reading them with a pumpkin-decorated pointer!

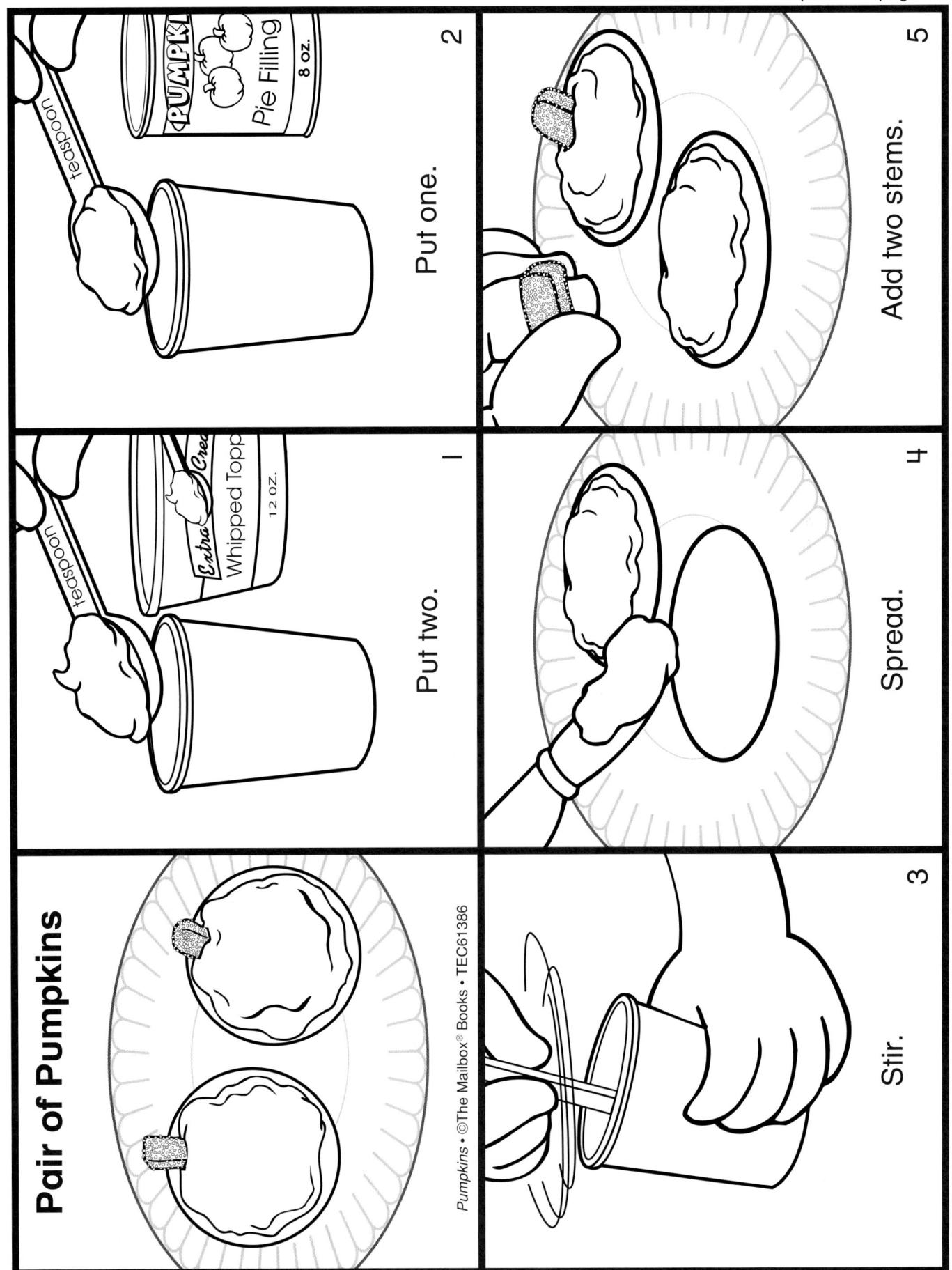

Recipe Cards
Use with "Pair of Pumpkins" on page 34.

Pumpkin Picture Cards
Use with "In the Pumpkin Patch" on page 23.

Pumpkin Pattern
Use with "Toothy Grins" on page 26 and "Pumpkin Stack" on page 28.

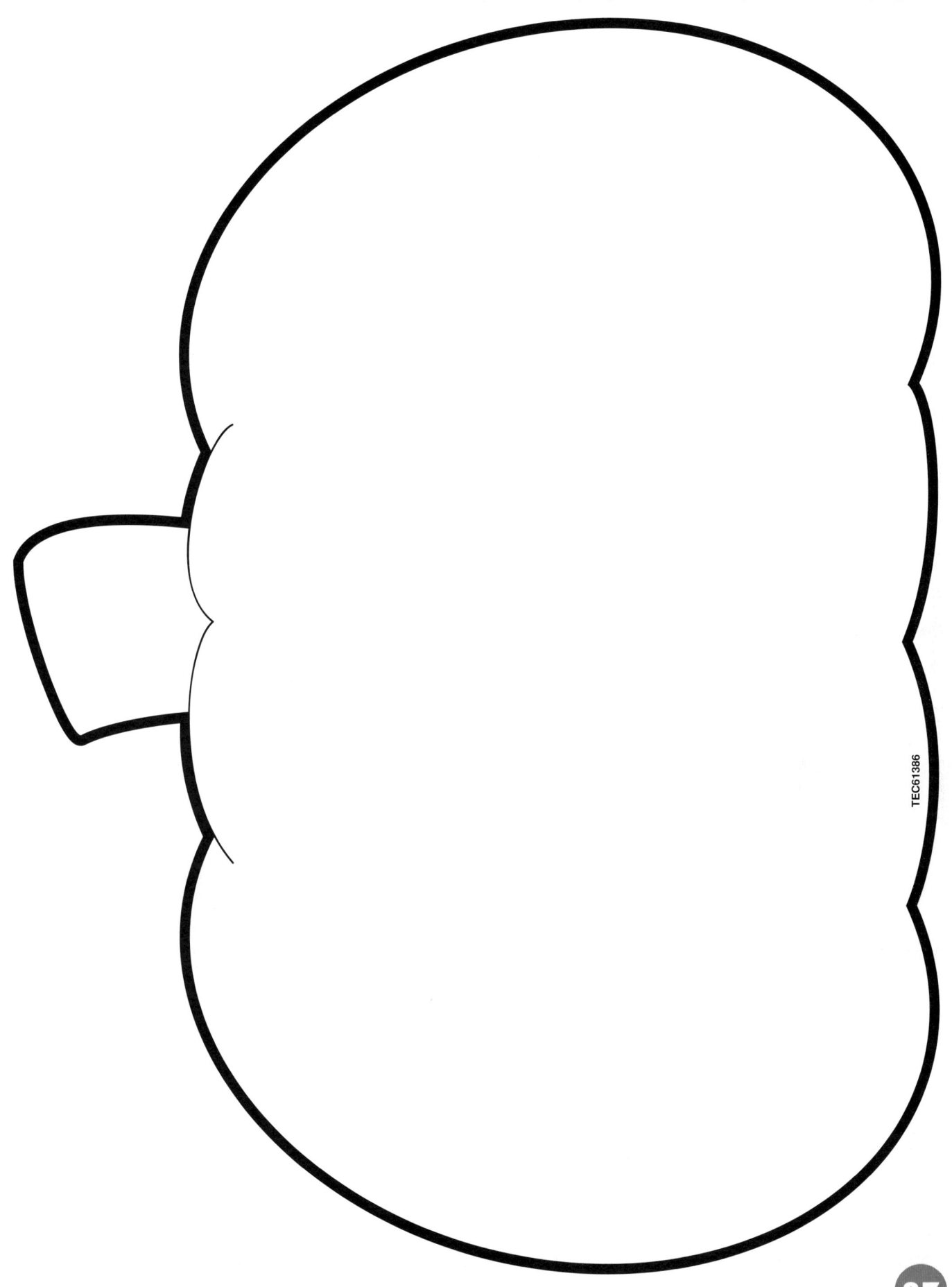

Book Report Form

Use with "The Book Patch" on page 33.

Name ______________________________

Title: ______________________________

Author: ______________________________

The best part of the story was when ______________

____

____

Pumpkin-Seed Book Rating

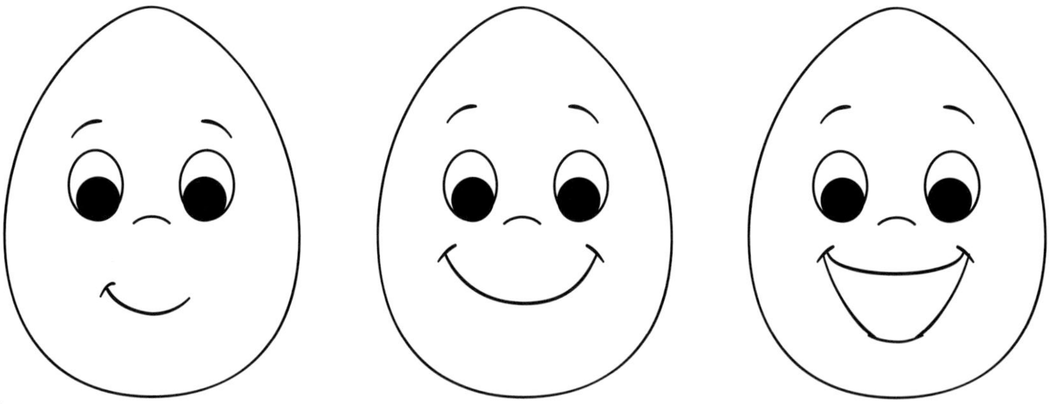

okay **good** **great**

TEC61386

"How a Pumpkin Grows" Booklet

How to Use Pages 40–43

Use this booklet to introduce or review the life cycle of a pumpkin. Give each child a copy of pages 40, 41, 42, and 43. Read the text aloud to youngsters and then help them follow the directions below to complete the booklet.

Directions for Each Student

1. Booklet cover: Write your name. Color the cover and then cut it out.
2. Booklet pages 1–5: Color and cut out the pages and patterns. Glue the patterns in the spaces provided.
3. Booklet page 6: Color the page and cut out the large pumpkin.
4. Sequence the booklet cover and pages on top of the pumpkin and staple them together along the top.

Finished Sample

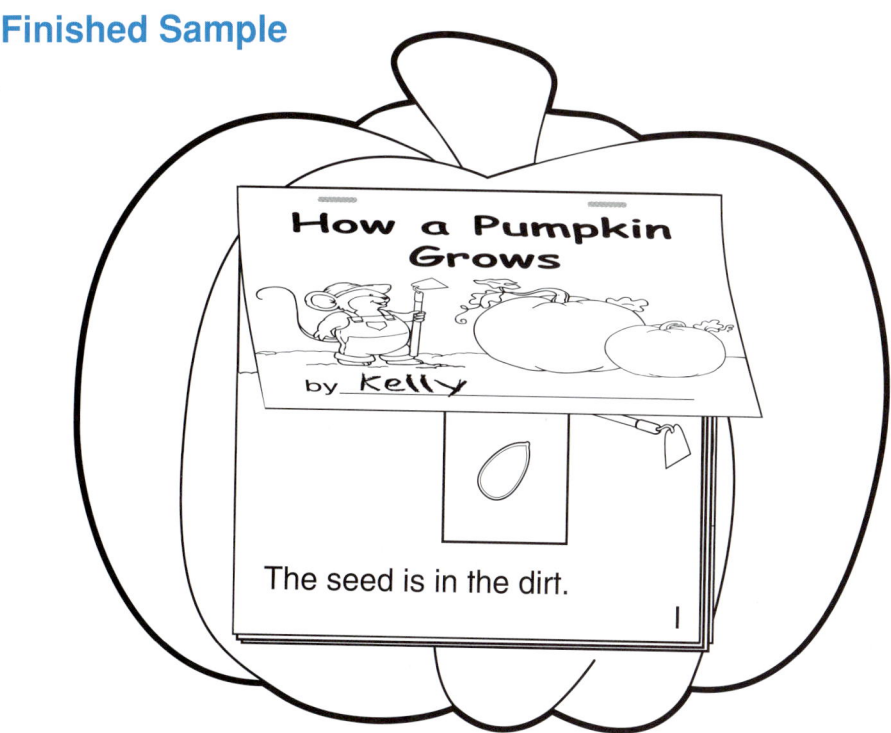

Pumpkin Life Cycle
Booklet cover and page 1: seed

How a Pumpkin Grows

by _____

Pumpkins • ©The Mailbox® Books • TEC61386

The seed is in the dirt.

1

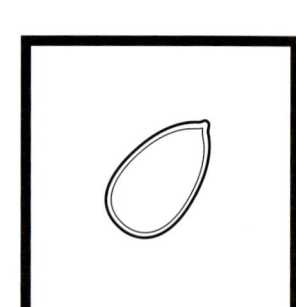

Pumpkin Life Cycle
Booklet pages 2 and 3: sprout and vine

The seed begins to sprout.

2

The sprout grows into a vine.

3

Pumpkin Life Cycle

Booklet pages 4 and 5: flower and small pumpkin

A flower grows on the vine.

4

A pumpkin grows on the vine.

5

Pumpkin Life Cycle
Booklet page 6: pumpkin

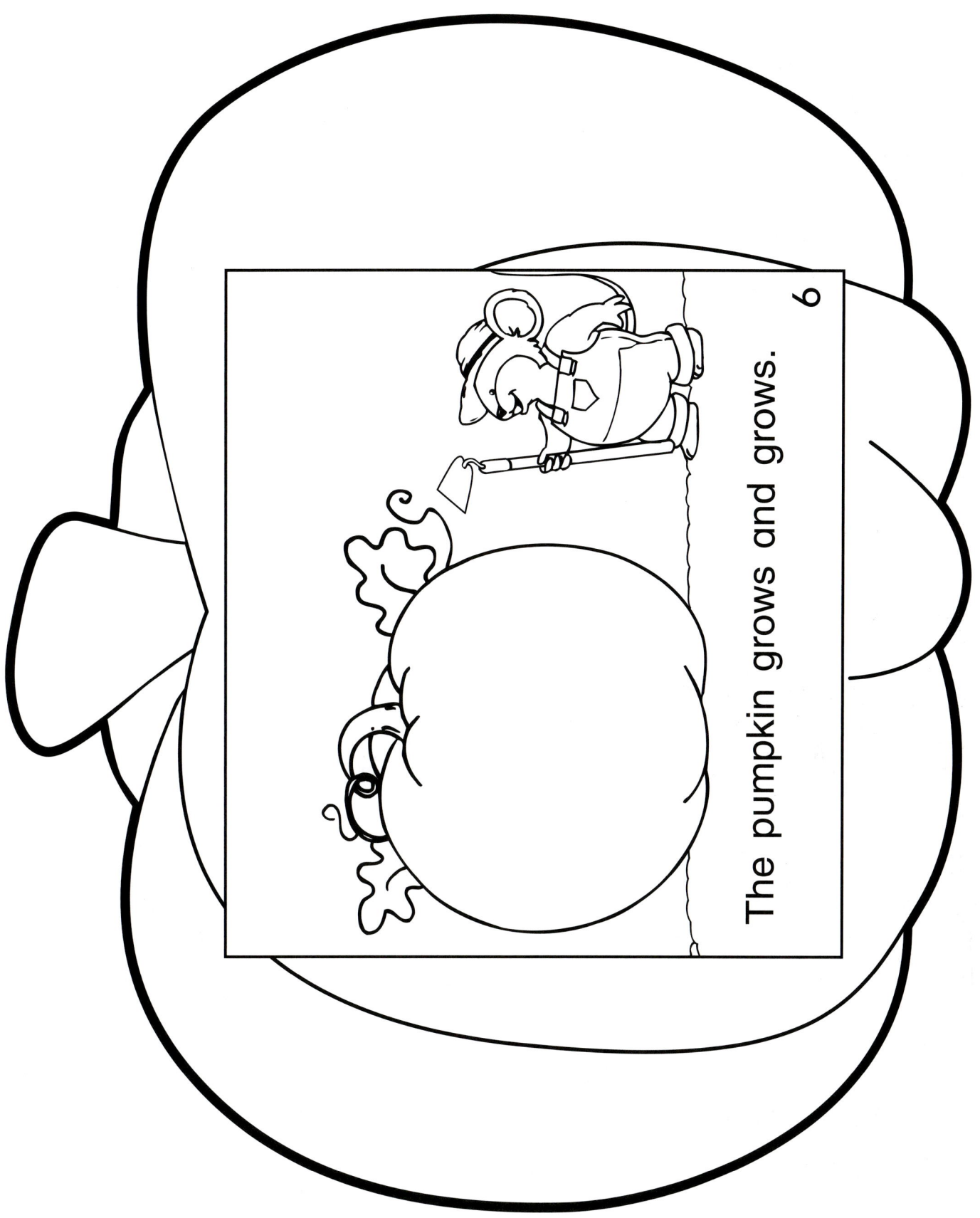

Beginning Letters and Sounds
h, l, p

Name _____

Tending the Patch

Cut.
Glue to match the beginning sounds.

Name _____

Beginning Letters and Sounds
m, t

Up on Top

🖍 Color by the code.

Color Code

begins with **m** like 🧹 — orange

begins with **t** like 👔 — yellow

Name _____

Sets/more

Bring in the Harvest

Count the pumpkins in each side of the barn.
🖍 Color the set that has **more**.

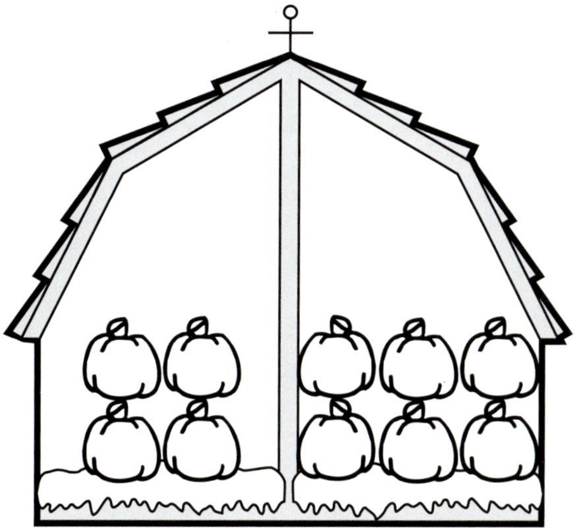

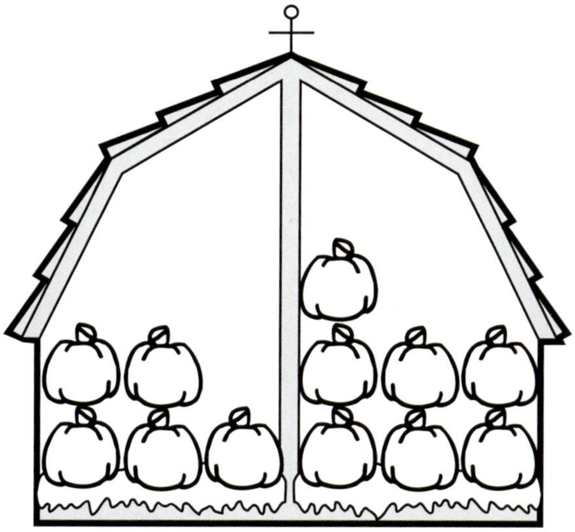

47

Name _____   Counting 1–6

Pick of the Patch

Count the seeds.

Cut. Glue the numbers.

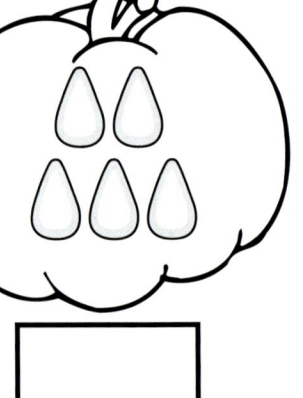

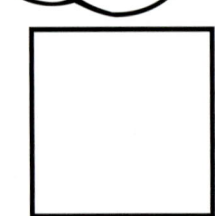

| 1 | 2 | 3 | 4 | 5 | 6 |

48